4th Edition

WORK WITH ENGLISH

von
Steve Williams

in Zusammenarbeit mit der
Verlagsredaktion

Cornelsen

Verfasser: Steve Williams, Corio Bay Media; Melbourne

Projektleitung: Jim Austin
Verlagsredaktion: Kari-ann Seamark
Layout und technische Umsetzung: EYES-OPEN, Berlin
Umschlaggestaltung: Klein & Halm Grafikdesign, Berlin
Titelfotos: Shutterstock (10) Alamy RF/juice Images (1)

Erhältlich sind auch:

Allgemeine Ausgabe:	
Schülerbuch	ISBN 978-3-06-520517-7
Workbook mit Audio-CD	ISBN 978-3-06-520520-7
Workbook mit CD-ROM und Audio-CD	ISBN 978-3-06-450640-4
Workbook mit Audio-CD Lehrerfassung	ISBN 978-3-06-520521-4
Handreichungen zum Unterricht mit Lehrer-CD und 3 Audio-CDs	ISBN 978-3-06-520519-1
Baden-Württemberg Ausgabe:	
Schülerbuch	ISBN 978-3-06-450612-1
Workbook mit Audio-CD	ISBN 978-3-06-450701-2
Workbook mit CD-ROM und Audio-CD	ISBN 978-3-06-450702-9
Workbook mit Audio CD Lehrerfassung	ISBN 978-3-06-450703-6
Handreichungen zum Unterricht mit Lehrer-CD und 3 Audio-CDs	ISBN 978-3-06-450700-5

www.cornelsen.de

1. Auflage, 1. Druck 2012

Alle Drucke dieser Auflage sind inhaltlich unverändert und können im Unterricht nebeneinander verwendet werden.

Druck: H. Heenemann, Berlin

ISBN 978-3-06-450641-1

Inhalt gedruckt auf säurefreiem Papier aus nachhaltiger Forstwirtschaft.

Inhaltsverzeichnis

Abbreviations and symbols

BE	British English
AE	American English
GB	Great Britain
US	USA
<>	opposite
v	verb
n	noun
adj	adjective

accent	He speaks with a Scottish accent.	Akzent
advantage	Speaking English is an advantage in many jobs.	Vorteil
advertising	There's a lot of advertising on the internet.	Werbung, Werbeabteilung
appointment	You need an appointment to see the doctor.	Termin
boss	If I'm late, my boss will be angry.	Chef/in
canteen	We often eat in the canteen.	Kantine
capital city	The capital city of France is Paris.	Hauptstadt
to celebrate	They had a party to celebrate.	feiern
to chat	He likes to chat with his friends.	sich unterhalten, chatten
to communicate	We often communicate by email.	kommunizieren
conversation	I had a long conversation with her.	Gespräch, Unterhaltung
customer	The customer bought a T-shirt.	Kunde/-in
department	I work in the IT department.	Abteilung
directions	I gave him directions to the station.	Wegbeschreibung
economy	The German economy is doing well.	Wirtschaft
entrance	<> exit	Eingang
fluent	She speaks fluent Spanish.	(*Sprache:*) fließend
foreign language	English is a foreign language for Germans.	Fremdsprache
globalization	Thanks to globalization we can buy goods from anywhere.	Globalisierung
to have lunch	We usually have lunch at 12.30.	zu Mittag essen
home	Africa is the home of lions and elephants.	Heimat, Zuhause
industry	We work in the film industry.	Branche, Industrie
island	Ireland is an island.	Insel
job interview	I had a job interview at the London office.	Vorstellungsgespräch
lift (*BE*)	*AE*: elevator	Aufzug
manufacturing	He works in car manufacturing.	Herstellung, Fertigung

map	Find Manchester on the map.	Landkarte, Karte
midnight	They stayed up until midnight.	Mitternacht
mostly	Our English lessons are mostly interesting.	hauptsächlich
to move	We moved to the US for my father's job.	*hier:* übersiedeln
native language	English is my native language.	Muttersprache
native speaker	Katie is a native speaker of English.	Muttersprachler/in
noon	The morning is over – it's already noon.	Mittag
nowadays	Nowadays most people use email.	heute, heutzutage
population	The population of the UK is about 60 million.	Bevölkerung
to practise	You have to practise if you want to do well.	üben, trainieren
present	Here's a present for your birthday.	Geschenk
to pronounce	How do you pronounce this word?	aussprechen
pronunciation	Listen carefully to the pronunciation of this word.	Aussprache
purse	She keeps her money in her purse.	Handtasche (*AE*), Portemonnaie (*BE*)
reason	Why are you late? There must be a reason.	Grund
reception	Please go to reception when you arrive.	Empfang
receptionist	He works as a receptionist in a hotel.	Empfangsmitarbeiter/in
sales	I want to work in sales because I like selling things.	Vertrieb, Verkauf(sabteilung)
stairs	Go up the stairs to the first floor.	Treppe
statement	Is that a statement or a question?	Aussage, Behauptung
translation	What's the German translation of this word?	Übersetzung
TV series	This TV series is on every evening.	Fernsehserie
voice	He has a loud voice.	Stimme
to vote	The people voted for a new president.	abstimmen, wählen

11/13

How much have you learned? Do the tasks to find out.
Only look at pages 4–5 if you are stuck.

1 Complete the crossword.

1 When two or more people talk to each other, it's called a …
2 When two or more people give each other information, they …
3 If you want to know where all the countries in the EU are, you can look at a …
4 The language that you learned as a baby is your … language.
5 When people talk to each other in an informal and friendly way, they …
6 If you speak a language well, you are … in it.
7 When you don't know what an English word means, you might look in a dictionary for a …
8 Because we often don't write English words phonetically, you also need to find out how to … them.
9 This is where you come from.
10 If you are German and live in Britain, you have to be able to speak a … language.
11 When you set a time and date to speak to someone, you make an …
12 You do this to mark a special occasion.

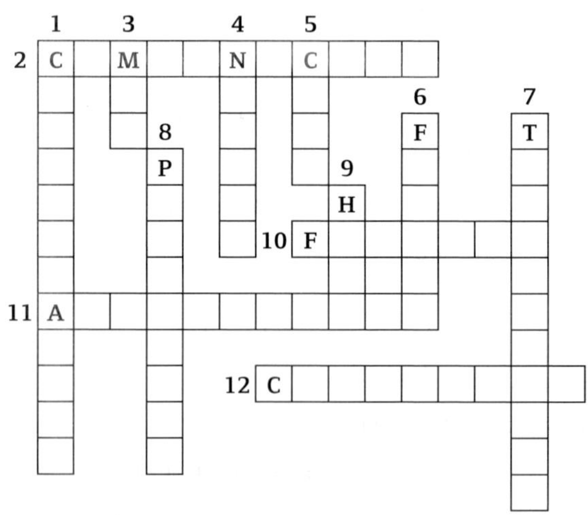

2 **Find the vowels to complete the missing words.**

1 Excuse me. I'm trying to find the park. Can you give me ______________________ DRCTNS, please?

2 A lot of ______________________ CSTMRS come into the shop each day to buy things.

3 I want to get into the building but I can't find the ________________ NTRNC.

4 ______________________ DVRTSNG tells you about products and tries to make you buy them.

5 We don't have a lift – please use the ________________ STRS.

6 That's my mum in the next room – I can tell by the sound of her _________ VC.

7 A long time ago, most people worked on the land. ______________________ NWDYS, most people live and work in the city.

8 James works in the sales _____________________ DPRTMNT of our company.

9 Berlin is the ___________________________ CPTL CTY of Germany.

10 When things go wrong, it's important to find out the _________________ RSN.

11 The only way to speak better English is to ____________________ PRCTS.

12 How many people live in the EU? – I don't know. I'm not sure what the ____________________________ PPLTN is.

13 Do you go out for lunch? – No, we stay here and eat in the office __________________ CNTN.

14 The __________________________ MNFCTRNG industry makes things.

15 Because she speaks with a strong __________________ CCNT, it's difficult to understand her.

16 I know how to spell this word but I'm not sure about its ________________________ PRNNCTN.

17 It's Jim's birthday but I didn't buy him a ____________________ PRSNT.

18 I can't find my __________________ PRS – all my money is in it!

19 Is that a film? – No, it's a TV ________________ SRS: it's on every Tuesday.

20 It can be an ________________________ DVNTG to learn a second language early in life. It's often more difficult later.

adopted	I was adopted: I don't know my real mother.	adoptiert
adult	<> child	Erwachsene/r
advertisement	*AE*: commercial	Werbespot
asylum	He came to Germany as an asylum seeker.	Asyl
aunt	Aunt Lucy is my mother's sister.	Tante
background	My ethnic background is complicated.	Herkunft
bilingual	I'm bilingual in German and English.	zweisprachig
to book	I'd like to book a hotel room, please.	buchen, reservieren
citizen	She's an EU citizen: she has an EU passport.	Staatsbürger/in
colleague	These are my colleagues: we work together.	Kollege/-in
company	The small company had 10 employees.	Firma, Unternehmen, Gesellschaft
credit card	I used my credit card to buy new clothes.	Kreditkarte
to criticize	Don't criticize me: you couldn't do better.	kritisieren
details	Please fill in your contact details on the form.	Angaben, Daten
dream	It's my dream to live in Australia.	Traum
education	All children in Germany are able to get a free education.	Schulbildung, Ausbildung
enormous	That's an enormous piece of cake!	enorm, gewaltig
flat (*BE*)	*AE*: apartment	Wohnung
free	It doesn't cost anything: it's free.	kostenlos, gratis
to give sth up	I'm going to give up cigarettes.	etw aufgeben
government	The government should do more for poor people.	Regierung
grandmother	My grandmother lived to the age of 87.	Großmutter
grandparents	Ella's grandparents are nearly 70.	Großeltern
guest	Of course you can't pay: you're my guest.	Gast
husband	He's not my boyfriend, he's my husband.	Ehemann
to imagine sth	Just imagine if you were an airline pilot.	sich etw vorstellen
immigrant	There are a lot of Turkish immigrants in Germany.	Einwanderer/-in

meeting	We need to have a meeting to discuss this.	Sitzung, Besprechung
member	Are you a member of the club?	Mitglied
noisy	<> quiet	laut
passport	You need a passport to travel to other countries.	Pass, Reisepass
to pick sb up	I'll pick you up at the station.	jdn abholen
to pick sth	Pick any colour you like.	etw auswählen
to receive	<> to give	erhalten, bekommen
refugee	My grandfather left Germany in 1938 as a refugee.	Flüchtling
relative	You can choose your friends but not your relatives.	Verwandte/r
to replace	Is it broken? Don't worry: I'll replace it.	ersetzen, austauschen
to reserve	Can I reserve a table in the restaurant, please?	reservieren
rural	It's the rural life for me: I love the countryside.	ländlich
to share sth	Don't eat all of it – share it with me!	(sich) etw teilen
siblings	I have two siblings: a brother and a sister.	Geschwister
single parent	My mum is a single parent: my dad left home.	Alleinerziehende/r
stepmother	She's my stepmother, my father's new wife.	Stiefmutter
surname	The authors' surnames are Ashdown and Williams.	Nachname
terrible	That was a terrible joke: it wasn't funny at all.	furchtbar
uncle	Uncle Bob is my dad's brother.	Onkel
urban	I like urban life – the city is fun!	städtisch, Stadt-
vegetarian	I'm a vegetarian: I gave up meat 3 years ago.	Vegetarier/in
war	Thousands of people died in the war in Iraq.	Krieg
to welcome sb	The boss welcomed him to the company.	jdn willkommen heißen
wife	I'm Barry Jones and this is my wife, Edna Jones.	Ehefrau
to wish	I wish it was Sunday and I could stay in bed.	wünschen
wonderful	That's a wonderful idea! Well done!	wunderbar

17/9

> How much have you learned? Do the tasks to find out.
> Only look at pages 8–9 if you are stuck.

1 **Work out the anagrams and complete the grid to find out what Paul's dream is.**

Paul and his family are EFUGERES[1]. They left their home country because of a terrible RAW[2]. They came to Germany and now they want to apply for SUMALY[3]. It is difficult for them because they do not have PORSASPTS[4]: they lost everything when they left their home country.

As RINGITAMSM[5] in Germany they find everything strange and new. They are learning German but it is not easy to learn a new language. Slowly they are making friends but some people do not MCWEOLE[6] more foreign guests. Some REZICICTI[7] them because they have a different culture and a different ethnic NAGKUDCOBR[8].

1	☐	☐	☐	☐	☐ 1	☐	☐ 2	☐		
2	☐	☐	☐ 3							
3	☐	☐	☐	☐	☐	☐ 4				
4	☐	☐ 5	☐	☐	☐	☐	☐	☐	☐	
5	☐	☐	☐	☐	☐	☐	☐	☐ 6	☐	☐
6	☐	☐	☐	☐ 7	☐	☐	☐			
7	☐	☐	☐ 8	☐ 9	☐ 10	☐	☐	☐ 11	☐ 12	
8	☐	☐	☐	☐	☐	☐	☐	☐	☐ 13	☐

Paul's dream is to become a

☐	☐	☐	☐	☐	☐		☐	☐	☐	☐	☐	☐	☐
1	2	3	4	5	6		7	8	9	10	11	12	13

2 **Find the following words in the word square. Write the German meaning next to each word.**

10 words about family

____________________ ____________________

____________________ ____________________

____________________ ____________________

____________________ ____________________

____________________ ____________________

____________________ ____________________

____________________ ____________________

____________________ ____________________

____________________ ____________________

____________________ ____________________

4 words about the world of work

____________________ ____________________

____________________ ____________________

____________________ ____________________

____________________ ____________________

A	S	T	R	A	W	I	F	E	D	R	I	S
R	I	G	R	A	N	D	P	A	R	E	N	T
M	B	R	A	D	K	R	I	L	L	U	U	E
E	L	I	C	O	M	P	A	N	Y	N	T	P
E	I	G	U	P	U	P	Y	S	H	C	R	M
T	N	H	R	T	R	O	L	U	F	L	W	O
I	G	U	D	E	D	F	I	R	E	E	R	T
N	O	N	S	D	R	A	U	N	T	E	E	H
G	I	D	D	L	R	E	L	A	T	I	V	E
A	H	U	S	B	A	N	D	M	A	W	I	R
A	D	V	E	R	T	I	S	E	M	E	N	T
W	O	R	C	O	L	L	E	A	G	U	E	D

attitude	What's your attitude towards nuclear energy?	Einstellung, Haltung
to avoid	Try to avoid making the teacher angry!	vermeiden, meiden
to ban	The school plans to ban mobile phones.	verbieten
to behave	The students behaved well in class.	sich verhalten, sich benehmen
career	After school, she started her career in sales.	Karriere
to cause	What caused this problem?	verursachen
cheap	<> expensive	billig
climate change	Scientists met to discuss climate change.	Klimawandel
comfortable	These jeans are old but comfortable.	gemütlich, bequem
decade	10 years	Jahrzehnt
definitely	<> possibly	bestimmt, absolut
disappointed	*n* disappointment	enttäuscht
to earn	She earns €50,000 a year.	verdienen
excitement	*adj* exciting	Aufregung, Spannung
fashion	In the 1960s, floral shirts were the fashion.	Mode
to fit	These jeans don't fit me, they're too big.	passen
to find out	How do we find out the answer to this question?	herausfinden
to grow up	Granddad grew up in the 1970s.	erwachsen werden
hard-working	<> lazy	fleißig, hart arbeitend
to improve	<> to get worse	verbessern, (sich) bessern
jacket	It was cold outside so I wore a jacket.	Jacke
to kill	The fire killed 10 people.	töten
leather	Are these shoes made of leather?	Leder
to look after sb/sth	The babysitter looked after the children.	sich um jdn/etw kümmern
to look sth up	Look up the word in the word list.	etw nachschlagen

lyrics	I like the song but the lyrics are silly.	Liedtext
mobile phone (*BE*)	*AE*: cell phone	Handy, Mobiltelefon
nuclear	Is nuclear energy safe?	Atom-
optimism	<> pessimism	Optimismus
politics	What started your interest in politics, President Obama?	Politik
power	Power to the people!	Kraft, Energie
pressure	The exams are putting us under pressure.	Druck
to put sb down	Stop putting me down: I'm doing my best.	jdn demütigen
relaxing	This music is very relaxing.	erholsam
sales assistant	I worked as a sale assistant in a supermarket.	Verkäufer/in
to save sth	We've saved € 2,000 for our holiday so far.	etw sparen
to seem	Granddad seems younger than 80.	scheinen
serious	Stop playing around and be serious!	ernst, ernsthaft
to settle down	I'm too young to settle down.	sesshaft werden
shirt	I wear a shirt and tie to work every day.	Hemd
silly	10.30? Don't be silly, it's only 9.45!	albern, dumm
smart	Ben looked very smart on his first day at work.	schick
suit	When he worked in a bank, he wore a suit.	Anzug
sunglasses	I always wear sunglasses in the summer.	Sonnenbrille
to taste	This food tastes terrible!	schmecken
to throw sth away	Don't throw that away – we might need it.	etw wegwerfen
tight	These jeans are too tight: I can't get into them.	eng
to wear	*not:* to carry	(*Kleidung:*) tragen
work experience	I did 2 weeks' work experience in an office.	Praktikum
to work sth out	I'm sure we can work out the answer.	herausbekommen
to worry about sth	Don't worry about things you can't change.	sich um etw Sorgen machen

12/14

How much have you learned? Do the tasks to find out.
Only look at pages 12–13 if you are stuck.

1 Find in the word circle 11 words to do with clothing. Write the German meaning next to each word.

three adjectives

two verbs

six nouns

2 **Complete the sentences with the correct word from the box. You need some of them more than once.**

about · after · away · down · out · up

1 It seems as if some older people like to put kids ______________.

2 Be nice to your parents: they looked ______________ you when you were young.

3 He was very quiet as a child, but when he grew ______________, he became a famous singer.

4 There is no point in worrying ______________ the future.

5 If you want to find old friends, why don't you look them ______________ on Facebook?

6 Don't throw those old clothes ______________, Granddad! You can sell them.

7 Gerry Rafferty was a rockstar but he decided to settle ______________ in a quiet little town and forget about everything.

8 What's the meaning of life? Let me know if you work it ______________!

3 **Complete the sentences with the English translations of the words in brackets.**

1 Do you think we should ________________ nuclear power? (*verbieten*)

2 It's a good email but I think you can still ________________ it a little bit. (*verbessern*)

3 That's a ________________ film. I don't want to see it. (*albern*)

4 What sort of ________________ do you want when you leave school? (*Karriere*)

5 When did you get your first ________________? (*Handy*)

6 Buy two and ________________ 25%! (*sparen*)

7 I like the song but I don't really understand the ________________. (*Songtext*)

8 I'm not trying to ________________ a big sensation, I'm just talking about my generation. (*verursachen*)

9 Climate change is a ________________ problem – it's not funny. (*ernsthaft*)

10 My mum buys me ________________ jeans instead of the expensive ones that I like. (*billig*)

11 How can we ________________ some money to pay for our holiday? (*verdienen*)

12 Mmm! This pizza ________________ very good! (*schmecken*)

account	Do you have a Facebook account?	Konto
advice	Her teacher gave her some good advice.	Rat, Ratschlag
to allow	His parents didn't allow him to watch TV.	erlauben, gestatten
to annoy sb	That song annoys me: it's so bad!	jdn belästigen, nerven
to be afraid of sb/sth	Don't be afraid of the teacher – she's nice really.	vor etw Angst haben
bored	I'm bored: there's nothing to do.	gelangweilt
bully	Leave him alone, don't be a bully!	Mobber/in, Tyrann
choice	Stay or go, it's your choice.	Wahl, Entscheidung
comment	He wrote a comment on her Facebook page.	Kommentar, Bemerkung
to complain	Don't complain if things go wrong.	sich beschweren
to contact sb	She contacted him through Myspace.	Kontakt zu jdm aufnehmen
CV (*BE*)	*AE*: résumé	Lebenslauf
cyberbullying	Cyberbullying is a big problem in schools.	Mobbing im Internet
to delete	Please delete that stupid comment.	löschen
depressed	<> happy	niedergeschlagen, deprimiert
diary	I write in my diary every day.	Tagebuch
embarrassing	What a bad photo! That's embarrassing!	peinlich
employer	<> employee	Arbeitgeber/in
face-to-face	We had a face-to-face conversation.	persönlich
horrible	That's a horrible thing to say.	schrecklich
to hurt sb	The nasty remark hurt him.	jdn verletzen
insecure	<> secure, safe	unsicher
insult	Work for € 10 an hour? That's an insult!	Beleidigung
to interest	That doesn't interest me at all.	interessieren
joke	He tells funny jokes.	Witz, Streich
to keep in touch	It's important to keep in touch with friends.	in Verbindung bleiben
lie	<> truth	Lüge

lonely	I feel lonely without my friends.	einsam
media	TV, radio and the internet are media.	Medien
message	What's the message of the film?	Botschaft
nasty	You shouldn't be nasty to people.	gemein, böse
network	It's a network of people with the same interests.	Netzwerk
personal	<> public, shared	persönlich, eigene/r/s
personality	She has a nice, friendly personality.	Persönlichkeit
popular	<> unpopular	beliebt
to post sth	I posted the photo on Facebook.	anschlagen, aushängen
privacy	You should protect your privacy online.	Privatsphäre
programme	My favourite programme is *Wetten das?*	Sendung
public	<> private	öffentlich
to remove	I removed that bad photo from my profile.	entfernen
to reply	Please reply to my email.	antworten
reputation	what people think of sb	Ruf, Ansehen
rude	The rude comment made him angry.	unhöflich, unverschämt
to scare sb	The horror film scared us.	jdm Angst einjagen, jdn verängstigen
shocked	I was shocked to hear the bad news.	schockiert
stranger	I don't know him: he's a stranger.	Fremde/r
text message	I got a text message on my phone.	SMS
threat	It's illegal to make threats online.	Drohung
to threaten	Don't threaten me!	drohen
to trust	Trust me: I'm your friend.	vertrauen
to upload	<> to download	hochladen
upset	She seemed unhappy and upset.	bestürzt, aufgeregt
user	There are 34 forum users online now.	Benutzer/in
victim	They were all victims of bullying.	Opfer
youth	It's a youth club – it's for people under 21.	Jugend

13/15

How much have you learned? Do the tasks to find out.
Only look at pages 16–17 if you are stuck.

1 **Complete the crossword.**

Online tips

1 When you … photos to the internet, make sure they're not too big.
2 If you don't protect your … , someone else could steal your information.
3 If you write a … on a friend's photo, don't write anything which might hurt them.
4 Your … contains a lot of personal information. Don't let anyone else use it.
5 When people use online social … such as blogs and chatrooms, they don't always behave as well as they do face-to-face.
6 If someone writes something rude on your personal web page, just … it: don't reply.
7 Remember that … is illegal as well as nasty: don't do it.
8 Always respect other internet … . Nobody likes a bully!
9 Don't just use big social … like Facebook, try smaller ones as well.
10 If you want people to read your … , make it quite short.

2 **Complete the words.**

1 When I heard the bad news, I felt up________________.

2 He didn't think he was good enough: he was quite in________________.

3 My brother is a very bad dancer – it's really em________________ to go to discos with him.

4 What she wrote on my Facebook page an________________ me. Why did she write that?

5 It would be a good idea to re________________ that mobile phone from your desk before the teacher sees it.

6 Thanks for calling. I was feeling a bit de________________ but now I feel happy.

7 My boss is a good em________________ – he treats us all well.

8 Don't com________________ – things could be a lot worse!

9 Listen to my ad________________ : don't trust him.

10 If you want to con________________ her, send her an email.

3 **Read the clues and complete the words.**

1 It's a show on TV or radio. p________________

2 It's the opposite of private. p________________

3 You shouldn't tell these – tell the truth instead! l________________

4 If this is how you feel, you should do something interesting. b________________

5 You usually have at least two of these. Which one will you pick? c________________

6 If you read this later, you can find out what you did and thought. d________________

7 It's meant to be funny. j________________

8 It isn't nice to get one of these. i________________

9 Everyone is one of these until you get to know them. s________________

10 It doesn't last for ever so enjoy it while you can! y________________

addicted to	He is addicted to drugs	süchtig nach, abhängig von
to appear	She appeared happy but she was depressed.	scheinen, erscheinen
attention	Madonna gets a lot of media attention.	Aufmerksamkeit
celebrity	The celebrity had many fans.	Prominente/r, Promi
to change	Do I have to change?	(*Züge usw.*) umsteigen
channel	Which TV channel are you watching?	Kanal
comparison	Make a comparison between the shows.	Vergleich
to compete	He competed in the Olympic Games.	konkurrieren
contestant	There are 10 contestants in the quiz show.	Kandidat/in
dangerous	Drinking too much alcohol is dangerous.	gefährlich
to depart	The train departs at 6.37 p.m.	abfahren, abreisen
departure	<> arrival	Abfahrt, Abreise
to dislike	I dislike reality shows, they're terrible.	nicht mögen
drug	Say no to drugs!	Droge, Drogen-
to exercise	He's fit because he exercises a lot.	sich körperlich betätigen
fame	People on reality shows often want fame.	Ruhm
furniture	There is a lot of furniture in this house.	Möbel
glamorous	The life of the rich seems really glamorous.	glamourös
happiness	Money can't buy happiness.	Zufriedenheit, Glück
headline	Lady Gaga is in the headlines today.	Überschrift
to hide	I can't hide my feelings any longer.	verbergen, verheimlichen
huge	That's a huge mistake. Why didn't you see it?	riesig, gewaltig
to insult sb	Don't insult people – it isn't nice.	jdn beleidigen
to involve	What does this game involve?	beinhalten, einbeziehen
journey	It's a long journey from Munich to Berlin.	Fahrt, Reise
keyboard	iPads don't have a keyboard.	Tastatur
to make sth up	It isn't true: you made it up!	sich etw ausdenken, etw erfinden

marriage	Hollywood marriages are often short.	Ehe
miserable	He looks happy but really he's miserable.	unglücklich, elend
obese	She ate so much that she became obese.	fettleibig
old-fashioned	<> modern	altmodisch
performance	That was Brad Pitt's best performance.	Leistung, Darbietung, Aufführung
plastic surgery	He looked younger after plastic surgery.	kosmetische Chirurgie
platform	The train leaves from platform 4.	Bahnsteig, Gleis
printer	The computer can't find a printer.	Drucker
prize	I won a prize for my photograph.	Preis, Gewinn
rehab	He spent 2 months in drug rehab.	Entzug
safely	You can't take drugs safely.	sicher
scandal	The newspaper wrote about the scandal.	Skandal
scientist	Albert Einstein was a famous scientist.	(Natur-) Wissenschaftler/in
seat	Is this seat free?	Platz, Sitz
secretly	They got married secretly – nobody knew.	heimlich
shelf, shelves	Put the books on the shelf.	Regal, Regale
shocking	The news of the tsunami was shocking.	schockierend
skill	Speaking English is an important skill.	Fähigkeit, Fertigkeit
smart	That was a smart idea – well done!	intelligent, clever
stationery	Get some pens from the stationery store.	Schreibwaren, Briefpapier
successful	The show was successful – 10 million people watched it.	erfolgreich
ticket machine	Does the ticket machine take credit cards?	Fahrkartenautomat
tragic	Michael Jackson's unhappy life was tragic.	tragic
trainee	The company will take on 10 trainees.	Auszubildende/r
trip	Let's go on a trip around the world.	Reise
TV show	Stromberg is a popular TV show.	Fernsehsendung, -serie
voicemail	Please leave a voicemail message.	Anrufbeantworter

23/4

How much have you learned? Do the tasks to find out.
Only look at pages 20–21 if you are stuck.

1 **Read the clues and complete the word grid to find something that a lot of Hollywood actors have.**

1 How well an actor does in a film or a play.
2 This is a person who everybody knows.
3 Most singers and actors want this.
4 The Simpsons is one. (2 words)
5 This is someone who tries to win on a reality show.
6 This is what he or she wants to win.
7 There is one of these when the media finds out something shocking.
8 Everybody wants to be this, in one way or another.
9 Rich people can have this kind of life.
10 If someone is addicted to something, they can go here.
11 These are what they may be addicted to.
12 These are the big titles in the newspapers.
13 An event or situation is this if it is very sad and ends badly.
14 If you do something this way, you hope that nobody will find out.

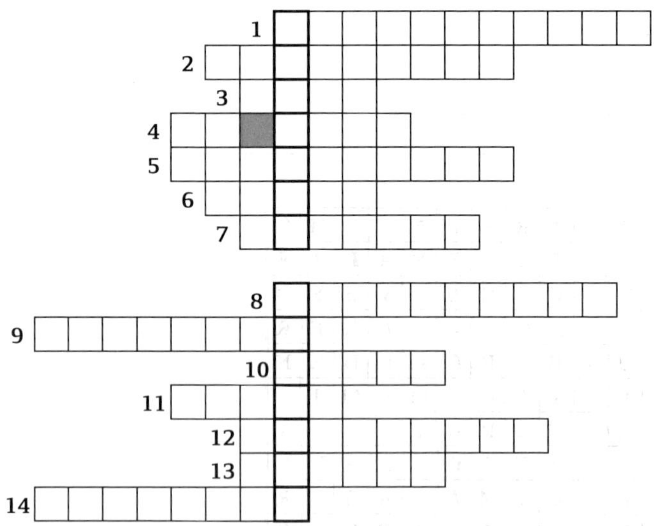

2 **Find the words in the word square. Write the German meaning next to each word.**

Travel

Two verbs

______________________ ______________________

______________________ ______________________

Five nouns (one has two words)

______________________ ______________________

______________________ ______________________

______________________ ______________________

______________________ ______________________

______________________ ______________________

The office

Six nouns for people and things you find there

______________________ ______________________

______________________ ______________________

______________________ ______________________

______________________ ______________________

______________________ ______________________

______________________ ______________________

G	E	A	T	T	R	I	P	A	N	T	H	O
J	R	R	U	I	Z	D	E	P	A	R	T	F
O	I	T	F	C	S	H	E	L	V	E	S	U
U	C	H	J	K	M	A	R	G	A	R	E	R
R	K	U	K	E	Y	B	O	A	R	D	N	N
N	P	L	A	T	F	O	R	M	E	M	I	I
E	G	R	E	M	G	R	O	Y	S	A	D	T
Y	P	S	T	A	T	I	O	N	E	R	Y	U
S	A	L	L	C	Y	M	A	D	A	G	E	R
U	L	F	R	H	I	C	H	A	T	R	L	E
S	T	R	A	I	N	E	E	S	Y	L	V	I
A	N	D	R	N	E	C	H	A	N	G	E	W
W	I	L	F	E	R	P	R	I	N	T	E	R

ability	The ability to speak English is important for this job.	Fähigkeit, Möglichkeit
to achieve sth	You achieve a lot if you believe in yourself.	etw erreichen
achievement	What a great achievement!	Errungenschaft, Erfolg
to afford sth	I can't afford this, it costs too much.	sich etw leisten (können)
to apply for sth	She applied for the job.	sich um etw bewerben
brand	What's your favourite brand of jeans?	Marke
to build	I want to build my own house.	bauen, aufbauen
to bully	Don't try to bully me – I'm not scared of you!	mobben, tyrannisieren
certificate	She got a certificate at the end of the course.	Urkunde, Zeugnis
childhood	<> adulthood	Kindheit
to come true	Maybe your dream will come true.	wahr werden, sich verwirklichen
creative	That's a really creative idea.	kreativ
determined	He's determined and tries hard.	entschlossen
disadvantage	<> advantage	Nachteil
to divorce	They divorced after 5 years of marriage.	sich scheiden lassen
doctor	I'm not well, I need a doctor.	Arzt/Ärztin
dreamer	He isn't a practical person, he's a dreamer.	Träumer
dyslexia	Dyslexia makes it hard to learn to read.	Legasthenie
effort	Make an effort – you can do this!	Mühe, Anstrengung
to employ sb	Why should we employ you?	jdn beschäftigen
experience	Do you have enough experience for this job?	Erfahrung
to fight	He had to fight to be successful.	kämpfen
flight	The Virgin flight leaves at 10.00.	Flug
fluent	He spoke fluent French.	fließend
to give away	Don't give it away, you need it.	(ver)schenken, spenden
goal	What are your goals in life?	Ziel
health	Health is more important than money.	Gesundheit

to inspire	My teacher inspired me to do well.	anregen, inspirieren
interviewee	The interviewee got the job.	Person, die interviewt wird
to matter	Don't worry, it doesn't matter.	wichtig sein
outdoors ✓	I work outdoors, in the fresh air.	draußen, im Freien
parent ✓	Come home and meet my parents.	Vater/Mutter, Elternteil
possibility ✓	You have to see the possibilities.	Möglichkeit
prediction	My prediction is that you will do well.	Voraussage, Vorhersage
primary school (*BE*)	*AE*: elementary school	Grundschule
to promote sb	They promoted her to manager.	jdn befördern
realistic ✓	Be realistic: it will be hard work.	realistisch
remarkable	It's a remarkable story.	bemerkenswert
risk ✓	It's a risk, I hope it'll be OK.	Risiko
secondary school (*BE*)	*AE*: high school	Hauptschule/ Realschule
to solve	Help me to solve this problem.	lösen
to start a company	Richard Branson has started many companies.	ein Unternehmen gründen
success	Finally he achieved success.	Erfolg
technical ✓	I like technical subjects like IT.	technisch
tough	It's tough but you can do it.	hart
to train as	He trained as a doctor.	eine Ausbildung zum/ zur … machen
training ✓	Her training got her a good job.	Ausbildung
vocational college	I got a job after leaving vocational college.	Berufsfachschule
voluntary	It's a voluntary job so I don't get paid.	freiwillig, ehrenamtlich
to waste	Don't waste your money on rubbish.	verschwenden, vergeuden
work placement	He did a two-week work placement.	Praktikum

13/11

How much have you learned? Do the tasks to find out.
Only look at pages 24–25 if you are stuck.

1 **Complete the sentences with the English translations of the words in brackets.**

1 Katja goes to a ______________________ in Freiburg im Breisgau. (*Berufsfachschule*)

2 You need money to ______________________ . (*ein Unternehmen gründen*)

3 Candidates who don't speak English have a big ______________________ . (*Nachteil*)

4 You can finish your ______________________ while you work for us. (*Ausbildung*)

5 Would you say that your German is ______________________ ? (*fließend*)

6 Have you thought about doing ______________________ work when you leave school? (*ehrenamtlich*)

7 I finished ______________________ at the age of 12. (*Grundschule*)

8 Her ______________________ were rich but that didn't help her as much as you think. (*Eltern*)

9 Jed finished ______________________ in California last year. (*Haupt-/Realschule*)

10 Two weeks ago they ______________________ Anna to a better position. (*befördern*)

11 Last year I did a two-week ______________________ in an architect's office. (*Praktikum*)

12 Oprah had a difficult ______________________ but she didn't let that stop her. (*Kindheit*)

13 Hopefully one day William's dream will ______________________ . (*wahr werden*)

14 His teachers' ______________________ was right: Richard became very successful. (*Vorhersage*)

15 Did you get a ______________________ when you completed the course? (*Urkunde*)

2 **Find the vowels to complete the missing words.**

1 This is something diffcult that you have done.

CHVMNT ______________________________

2 You can only get this by doing the job.

XPRNC ______________________________

3 This is something you want to do.

GL ______________________________

4 If you do this to someone, you give them a job.

MPLY ______________________________

5 You shouldn't do this to anything.

WST ______________________________

6 This isn't a realistic person.

DRMR ______________________________

7 You need to do this to a house before you can live in it.

BLD ______________________________

8 This is a chance that something will go wrong.

RSK ______________________________

3 **All of the words in the sentences below have at least one pair of double letters. Complete the words.**

1 Why did you decide to _ pp _ _ for the job?

2 Working _ _ _ _ oo _ _ is OK if it isn't cold or raining.

3 You're such a _ _ ll _ – he's much smaller than you!

4 Perhaps I can _ ff _ _ _ to go on a trip around the world one day.

5 We can all have _ _ cc _ ss in life. It means different things to different people.

6 It doesn't _ _ tt _ _ what race, culture or religion we belong to, we're all equal.

7 Do you think that there is a _ _ ss _ _ _ _ _ _ _ that I will get the job?

8 _ _ _ _ _ _ _ _ _ ee_ should arrive on time or they won't get the job.

analytical	A scientist needs good analytical skills.	analytisch
artist ✓	The artist drew a flower.	Künstler/in
artistic	He has a lot of artistic talent.	künstlerisch
to be passionate about sth	I'm passionate about helping others.	sich für etw leidenschaftlich begeistern
to care about sth	Don't you care about our planet?	am Herzen liegen
careers counsellor	The careers counsellor gave me some advice.	Berufsberater/in
caregiver	She's a caregiver for old people.	Pfleger/in
childminding	As an au pair you have to like childminding.	Kinderbetreuung
common	That's a common career mistake.	verbreitet, häufig
communicative	She isn't very communicative.	kommunikativ
community	I prefer to live in a small community.	Gemeinschaft, Gemeinde
computer science	Computer science was my best subject at school.	Informatik
construction	He works in the construction industry.	Bau, Hausbau
covering letter	Send a covering letter with your CV.	Anschreiben, Begleitschreiben
driver ✓	Aaron works as a bus driver.	Fahrer/in
excellent	That was an excellent meal, thanks!	ausgezeichnet
exciting	It was an exciting film.	aufregend, spannend
financial ✓	I want to work in the financial sector.	finanziell, Finanz-
further education	She went on to further education after school.	Weiterbildung
gap year	I took a gap year between school and work.	Jahr zwischen Schule und Studium bzw. Berufsanfang
healthy ✓	<> ill, sick	gesund
industrial ✓	Essen is an industrial city.	Industrie-, industriell

innovative	That's an innovative idea.	innovativ
internship	He got an internship with the company.	Praktikum
job advertisement	Read the job advertisement carefully.	Stellenanzeige
to manage sth	Could you manage the IT department?	etw verwalten
mechanic	The mechanic repaired our car.	(Kfz-)Mechaniker/in
offer	Thank you for your offer.	Angebot
organic	Organic food may be healthier for you.	Bio-, Öko-
outgoing	She likes people and is very outgoing.	kontaktfreudig
personnel	The company has 100 personnel.	Mitarbeiter, Personal
profession	What's your profession?	Beruf
programmer	Jo is a computer programmer.	Programmierer/in
promise	I'll do it: that's a promise.	Versprechen
reliable	Is he reliable? Can we trust him?	zuverlässig
responsibility	This is your responsibility, not mine.	Verantwortung, Verantwortlichkeit
responsible	We need someone responsible for the job.	verantwortungsbewusst
rule	Why do you always break the rules?	Regel, Vorschrift
to run sth	The family ran the business for years.	leiten, führen
satisfaction	My job gives me a lot of satisfaction.	Genugtuung
school-leaver	Not all school-leavers find a job right away.	Schulabgänger/in
strict	My boss is very strict.	streng
suggestion	Can I make a suggestion?	Vorschlag
supplier	Phone the supplier and get some more.	Zulieferer, Lieferant/in
to take care of sb/sth	Could you take care of sick people?	sich um jdn/etw kümmern
technically minded	IT people are usually technically minded.	technikinteressiert
tour guide	The tour guide showed them around Paris.	Reiseführer/in, Reiseleiter/in

How much have you learned? Do the tasks to find out.
Only look at pages 28–29 if you are stuck.

1 Solve the anagrams.

1 He's a very TALLAICYNA person. He always uses logic to work things out.

____

2 I like to do activities which use my SCAITRIT talents – painting, for example.

____

3 Sarah is very OMCEVNIMICUTA. She always tells me what she is thinking.

____

4 That was an LEXTENCEL piece of work. Well done!

____

5 This show isn't very NEGCIXIT. Let's see what's on another channel.

____

6 I want to work in an LUDINTARSI job, perhaps as a mechanic.

____

7 It's an VOANETINIV plan. Nobody has tried that before.

____

8 How BELRELIA is that information? Are you sure that it's right?

____

9 A INICAFALN job might be interesting – in a bank, perhaps.

____

10 We need an NIUGOGTO person who likes dealing with customers.

____

11 I'm SOPBIRNESEL and I work hard. What more do you need?

____

12 Jebediah. Is that a MONCOM name? It sounds quite unusual to me.

____

13 The rules are very CIRSTT. You mustn't break them.

____

2 **Complete the careers crossword.**

1 If you are in a job which requires training, you have one of these.
2 Somebody who looks after very young people works in this area.
3 This person looks after old or sick people.
4 This person does creative work.
5 These people fix motors and other machines (*Geräte*).
6 The people in this industry build things.
7 This person is on the road many hours a day.
8 This person writes software.

3 **Match the words which go together. Then write the German meaning of each phrase.**

1 careers	science	______________________
2 computer	letter	______________________
3 covering	guide	______________________
4 further	minded	______________________
5 job	education	______________________
6 technically	counsellor	______________________
7 tour	advertisement	______________________

to abolish	It's time to abolish that stupid rule.	abschaffen
abroad	You could work abroad, e.g. in the UK.	im/ins Ausland
accommodation	I need accommodation in London.	Unterkunft
to adapt to sth	Can you adapt to the new situation?	sich an etw anpassen
administrative	Office jobs involve administrative tasks.	Verwaltungs-
application	Please send a CV with your application.	Bewerbung
apprenticeship	An apprenticeship often lasts 3 years.	Lehre, Ausbildung
to attract	What attracted you to this job?	anziehen, anlocken
border	The train crossed the German-Austrian border.	Grenze
co-worker	I like my co-workers in the office.	Arbeitskollege/-in
complaint	We made a complaint about low pay.	Klage, Beschwerde
contract	Your contract runs for 24 months.	Vertrag
dissatisfied	Many employees are dissatisfied with their boss.	unzufrieden
diversity	Our community has great cultural diversity.	Vielfalt
to draw	I'll draw a map to show you where to go.	zeichnen
elderly	Elderly people are those over 65.	älter, alt
enthusiastic	She was enthusiastic about her new job.	begeistert
examination	You have to pass the examination to get in.	Prüfung
excited	I'm very excited about the party.	aufgeregt, begeistert
geographical	Western Europe is a geographical region.	geographisch
graph	The graph shows prices have risen by 50%.	Diagram, Grafik
habit	Smoking is a bad habit.	Gewohnheit
to have a day off	I'm tired, I need a day off.	einen Tag frei bekommen
host country	Find out everything you can about your host country.	Gastgeberland
knowledge	Test your knowledge with this quiz.	Wissen, Kenntnis(se)
level	I have a high level of motivation.	Niveau
machinery	We need a mechanic to fix the machinery.	Maschinen, Geräte

majority	<> minority	Mehrheit
to operate	How do you operate this machine?	bedienen
opportunity	This is a great opportunity to start a new career.	Möglichkeit, Gelegenheit, Chance
to overcome sth	We had to overcome some difficulties.	etw überwinden
percentage	What percentage want to work in the EU? – 50%	Anteil, Prozentsatz
permanent(ly)	<> temporarily	dauerhaft
position	Why are you the best person for this position?	Stelle, Stellung, Position
to predict	I can't predict what will happen.	vorhersagen
to regret	I regret that I didn't apply for the job.	bereuen
relaxed	<> stressed	entspannt
to relocate	We need you to relocate to New York.	umsiedeln, umziehen
rent	The rent for the flat is €250 a week.	Miete
to rise	That rent will rise to €260 next year.	steigen, ansteigen
school leaving certificate	What grade did you get in your school leaving certficate?	Schulabgangszeugnis
sick leave	You may have 2 weeks sick leave a year.	Krankheitsurlaub
sign	Shh! Be quiet! Can't you read the sign?	Schild
strength	My greatest strength is flexibility.	Stärke
stressful	Dealing with customers can be stressful.	anstrengend, stressig
to study	I want to study IT at college.	studieren
temporary	<> permanent	(*Stelle:*) befristet
unfamiliar	This word is unfamiliar: what does it mean?	unbekannt
vocational training	She did vocational training after school.	Berufsausbildung
wages	You'll get your wages once a month.	Lohn, Gehalt
weakness	His biggest weakness is lack of motivation.	Schwäche
to work overtime	We need you to work 5 hours overtime this week.	Überstunden machen

How much have you learned? Do the tasks to find out.
Only look at pages 32–33 if you are stuck.

1 **Work out the anagrams. Then complete the puzzle to find out where Fabian wants to work.**

1 Fabian wants to work DAORAB.
2 He will finish his RECPINTIPSHEPA soon.
3 After that he wants to enjoy the IVYSERTID of the European Union.
4 There are lots of RIPEPOTTOSUNI for young Germans to work in the EU.
5 He has already sent an PINCAPIOTAL to a company that he wants to work for.
6 It's for a PYRTOEMAR job as a chef.
7 The NOCTARCT is for one year.
8 If it all goes well, Fabian will think about moving MYPNENETARL.
9 He will only do that if his girlfriend Anja can TELROCEA too.
10 However, she isn't sure that she wants to live in an INRALIFMAU country.

1														
		5	1											
2														
								7		13				3
3														
	17						11							
4														
				9			4							
5														
	15			6										
6														
		2												
7														
							8							
8														
										14				
9														
	12													
10														
		16	10											

1	2	3	4	5	6	7	8		9	10		11	12	13	14	15	16	17

2 **Read the definitions and then complete the words.**

1 To do with running a company, school, etc. a~~ccomodation~~ accomodation

2 What you make when you are unhappy with how someone did something c________

3 How you feel when something didn't go as well as you expected dissapointed

4 How you feel when you really want to do something enthusiastic

5 What you do to show how much you have learned e________

6 How you feel when something good is going to happen e________

7 A way of showing information g________

8 Something you do often h________

9 What you know k________

10 All kinds of machines m________

11 Most of the things/people in a group m________

12 How many out of a hundred p________

13 How strong you are s________

14 Making you worried and tired s________

3 **Choose the verb which best fits the context. There are three verbs that you don't need.**

abolish · adapt · attract · ~~draw~~ · have · operate · overcome · predict · regret · study · ~~work~~

1 Do you know how to ________ this machine?

2 I can't ________ his answers. He might say anything.

3 She may ________ that decision one day.

4 Do we have to use this data to draw a graph?

5 You look as if you need to work a day off.

6 I'm sure we can find a way to ________ those difficulties.

7 How often does he have to ________ overtime?

8 It isn't always easy to ________ to a different environment.

agreement	<> disagreement	Zustimmung
aim	What's the aim of this exercise?	Ziel
apology	I accept your apology. Don't do it again.	Entschuldigung
to attack	The boys attacked him in the park.	angreifen
to be suspicious of sb/sth	They're suspicious of things that are unfamiliar to them.	misstrauisch/argwöhnisch sein gegenüber
to be unlucky	You lose! Unlucky!	kein Glück haben
belief	We all have our own beliefs.	Glaube
brilliant	It's a brilliant place – you should go.	toll, super
to cancel	Sorry, we have to cancel the concert.	absagen, stornieren
cause	What was the cause of the fight?	Ursache, Grund
charity	The Red Cross is a global charity.	Wohltätigkeitsorganisation
compulsory	You have to do it – it's compulsory.	Pflicht-, obligatorisch
crime	Crime is rising in this town.	Verbrechen, Kriminalität
disability	Life with a disability is often difficult.	Behinderung
disabled	She was disabled after the accident.	behindert
to doubt	I doubt that it will rain today.	bezweifeln
enemy	<> friend	Feind
to feel uncomfortable	I feel uncomfortable about your suggestion.	sich unwohl fühlen
to get in trouble	They got in trouble with the police.	Ärger/Schwierigkeiten bekommen
to get involved in	Don't get involved in drugs.	mit etw zu tun haben, in etw hineingeraten
gun	The cowboy took out his gun.	Pistole, Gewehr
head teacher	I'll complain to the head teacher.	Schulleiter/in
ignorance	Racism is caused by ignorance.	Ignoranz, Unwissen
to illustrate	That illustrates what I was saying.	illustrieren
individual	I'm just one individual, what can I do?	Einzelperson
to judge	Don't be so quick to judge people.	(*hier:*) verurteilen

to justify	How can you justify nasty comments?	begründen, rechtfertigen
kind	She's a kind, friendly person.	nett, freundlich
lifestyle	After she won € 1 million, her lifestyle changed.	Lebensweise
to make a stand	We must make a stand and stop this.	für etw eintreten
murder	I read about the murder in the paper.	Mord
murderer	The police have caught the murderer.	Mörder/in
to offend	Some drug users often offend again.	straffällig werden
to persuade	How can I persuade you not to do it?	überzeugen, überreden
to prevent	How can we prevent more deaths?	verhindern, vorbeugen
qualification	He left school with no qualifications.	Abschluss, Qualifikation
racism	There is no place for racism in our community.	Rassismus
to realise	He realised that he was wrong.	klar werden, bewusst werden
to reduce	How can we reduce crime levels?	reduzieren, senken
rivalry	There was rivalry between the teams.	Rivalität
to run	Who runs the training course?	etw anbieten, durchführen
to shoot sb	The policeman shot him in the arm.	auf jdn schießen, jdn erschießen
to sign up	Will you sign up for this course?	sich anmelden
solution	That's the solution to the problem.	Lösung
staff	Twenty staff work in this company.	Mitarbeiter
to suit	9 a.m. doesn't suit me. How about 10?	passen
to throw sb out	Stop shouting or I'll throw you out of the club.	jdn hinauswerfen
victim	The victim had to go to hospital.	Opfer
violence	There is too much violence on our streets.	Gewalt
weak	<> strong	schwach

How much have you learned? Do the tasks to find out.
Only look at pages 36–37 if you are stuck.

1 **Complete the crossword.**

1 There was … when the two rival groups of football fans met.
2 Danielle was the latest … of a drugs war.
3 Perhaps the … is to put more police officers on our streets.
4 'Stop, or I'll have to … you,' warned the policeman.
5 After they leave the gang, teenagers don't usually … again.
6 We must … young children from joining gangs.
7 The newspapers have reported another … . That's the third death this month.
8 They … people on the street and take their money.
9 'If you mix with the wrong people, you'll get in …,' said David's mum.
10 The … wrote an apology to the parents of the girl who died.
11 According to this graph, … levels are rising. There is more illegal activity than before.
12 If we don't know the … of the problem, it's difficult to solve it.
13 Unlike in Germany, British police officers do not carry… .
14 When will the government … that something needs to change?

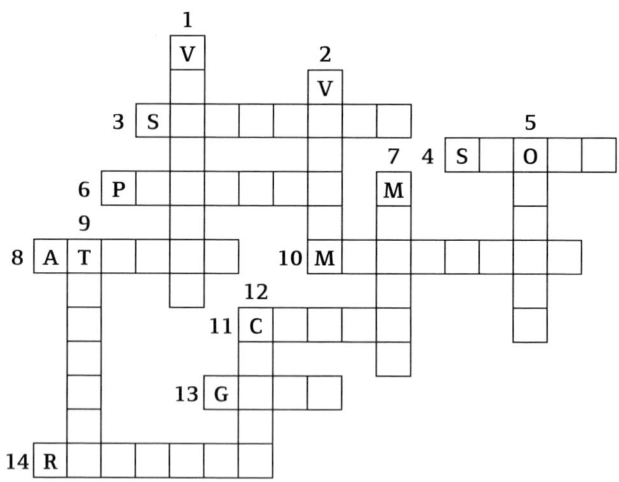

2 Solve the anagrams.

1 It's difficult to accept that our MEENIES are people just like us but it's true.

____

2 Unity was a TIRLABLIN idea – why can't we have more great ideas like that?

____

3 The government tried to FYJITSU the war but there was no good reason for it.

____

4 I try to respect the SEBFELI of others, even if I don't share them.

____

5 At first the teenage boy felt MONOBRUFTACEL around so many elderly people: he didn't know what to talk about.

____

6 People are often scared of those who have a different YLTEESILF to them.

____

7 The solution to MSARCI is better knowledge of other ethnic groups.

____

8 RIANNOECG of other cultures leads people to believe things that are not true.

____

9 Unfortunately we had to LACCEN the game because some players were ill.

____

10 She worked for a RAYCHTI which helped disabled young people.

____

11 Doesn't that LIATUSRELT the point I've just made?

____

12 We should never DEJUG anyone by how they look but we do it all the time.

____

13 It isn't easy to DUPERASE someone to leave a gang.

____

14 It's important to see the individual, not just the SITYBILIAD.

____

accident	It was an accident, I didn't mean to do it.	Unfall
action	You are responsible for your actions.	Handlung, Aktion
adventure	We love adventure.	Abenteuer
to affect	Alcohol affects your decisions.	etw beeinflussen, sich auf etw auswirken
to be addictive	Are computer games addictive?	süchtig machen
behaviour	The teacher criticized their bad behaviour.	Verhalten
change	Here's your change – 50 cents.	Wechselgeld
consequence	Think of the consequences of your actions.	Konsequenz
criminal record	If the police arrest you, you could get a criminal record.	Vorstrafenregister
criticism	I think your criticism is unfair.	Kritik
to depend on sb/sth	We all depend on our friends.	von jmdm/etw abhängen
to embarrass	Don't embarrass me in front of all these people!	jdn in Verlegenheit bringen, jdn bloßstellen
to endanger	Smoking endangers your health.	gefährden
entrepreneur	Richard Branson is an entrepreneur.	Unternehmer/in
foolish	That was a foolish thing to do.	dumm, leichtsinnig
fridge	Is there any milk in the fridge?	Kühlschrank
funfair	Let's go to the funfair.	Jahrmarkt, Rummel
to get off	We get off at the next station.	(*Zug etc.*:) aussteigen
health and safety	You have to wear a hat for health and safety.	Arbeitsschutz, Arbeitssicherheit
hooliganism	Football hooliganism is a big problem.	Rowdytum
human being	We're all human beings.	Mensch
to increase	The price of food has increased.	steigen
to injure	Careful! You'll injure someone.	verletzen
irresponsible	Driving too fast is irresponsible.	verantwortungslos
law	If you break the law, you'll get into trouble.	Gesetz(e), Recht
to lie (to sb)	Don't lie to me!	lügen, jdn belügen

obvious	It's obvious that you are lying.	klar erkennbar, offensichtlich
optimistic	I'm optimistic there won't be any problems.	optimistisch
overdose	He took an overdose and died.	Überdosis
pack	There are 12 tablets in a packet.	Packung
pain	I have a pain in my arm.	Schmerz(en)
painkiller	I need some painkillers.	Schmerzmittel
part-time	It's only a part-time job – 12 hours a week.	Teilzeit-
peers	Most people care what their peers think about them.	Gleichaltrige, Umgebung
pharmacy	Where's the nearest pharmacy, please?	Apotheke
to play it safe	Don't take risks – play it safe!	auf Nummer sicher gehen
police officer	I'm a police officer. Put down the gun.	Polizist/in
property	That's my property, keep your hands off!	Eigentum, Immobilie
to prove	Can you prove that you are over 16?	beweisen
range	She likes a range of extreme sports.	Reihe, Auswahl
receipt	Could I have a receipt, please?	Quittung
recent	Please include a recent photo of yourself.	jüngst
risky	That's too risky for me.	riskant
to ruin	Drugs can ruin your life.	zugrunde richten, ruinieren
safety gear	Don't forget to wear all the safety gear.	Sicherheitskleidung, -ausrüstung
shoplifting	They were caught shoplifting.	Ladendiebstahl
speed	Speed kills.	Geschwindigkeit
tablet	Take two tablets with water.	Tablette
terrifying	That horror film was terrifying.	furchterregend
thrill	We had lots of thrills at the funfair.	Nervenkitzel
unemployment	Unemployment in Germany is at 7%.	Arbeitslosigkeit
to vandalize	Some idiot has vandalized my car!	mutwillig beschädigen

S2

How much have you learned? Do the tasks to find out.
Only look at pages 40–41 if you are stuck.

1 **Find the words to describe 'risky behaviour' in the word square. Write the German meaning next to each word.**

M	E	M	T	E	R	R	I	F	Y	I	N	G	A
S	B	E	R	O	V	E	R	D	O	S	E	T	D
H	R	S	H	I	P	A	P	P	L	I	C	A	V
O	I	R	R	E	S	P	O	N	S	I	B	L	E
P	S	I	O	N	P	E	R	P	M	E	N	T	N
L	K	M	A	C	S	P	E	E	D	M	I	A	T
I	Y	A	D	D	I	C	T	I	V	E	L	T	U
F	I	V	A	N	D	A	L	I	Z	E	O	P	R
T	N	U	L	T	F	O	O	P	I	R	H	O	E
I	P	U	R	E	M	A	C	C	I	D	E	N	T
N	U	V	I	C	O	I	N	J	U	R	E	B	O
G	R	U	I	N	E	L	B	O	U	R	N	E	X

4 adjectives

______________________ ______________________

______________________ ______________________

______________________ ______________________

______________________ ______________________

3 nouns for actions

______________________ ______________________

______________________ ______________________

______________________ ______________________

2 nouns for consequences

______________________ ______________________

______________________ ______________________

3 verbs

______________________ ______________________

______________________ ______________________

______________________ ______________________

2 **Complete the sentences with the English translations of the words in brackets.**

1 Small amounts of alcohol ______________________ some people more than others, so it's better if you don't drink and drive. (*sich auswirken auf*)

2 You must study the ______________________ information before you start the job. (*Arbeitsschutz*)

3 Dan may get a ______________________ for writing graffiti tags. (*Vorstrafenregister*)

4 ______________________ have to take risks and make mistakes: there's no profit without pain! (*Unternehmer/innen*)

5 It will ______________________ her parents if she gets in trouble with the police. (*in Verlegenheit bringen*)

6 Which way the hang glider turns ______________________ where your body is. (*abhängen von*)

7 It's important to respect the ______________________ : you don't want to get into trouble, do you? (*Gesetz*)

8 It was ______________________ that she really enjoyed the hang gliding lesson. (*offensichtlich*)

9 When somebody vandalized Mr Jones' ______________________ , he felt depressed. (*Eigentum*)

10 The police can't ______________________ who wrote the graffiti on the bridge. (*beweisen*)

11 Because of the youth ______________________ in this city, a lot of young adults are bored and dissatisfied. (*Arbeitslosigkeit*)

12 All ______________________ make mistakes: that's OK if we learn from our experience. (*Menschen*)

13 The level of adrenaline ______________________ as the thrills get bigger. (*steigen*)

14 We all care what our ______________________ think, it's not just teenagers who think that way. (*Gleichaltrige, Umgebung*)

15 Did you see that ______________________ documentary about why young people take risks? (*jüngst*)

16 There is too much ______________________ of young people in the media. Everybody was young once, you know! (*Kritik*)

advertisement ✓	Did you read the advertisement?	Anzeige, Werbung
artificial	I prefer natural materials to artificial ones.	künstlich
bin	Please put rubbish in the bin.	Mülleimer, Mülltonne
bonus ✓	They got a bonus for the extra work.	Zulage
to breathe	I can hardly breathe in here.	atmen
button	A button has come off of my shirt.	Knopf
car park ✓	Leave your car in the car park.	Parkhaus, Tiefgarage
cloth	What cloth is this jacket made from?	Stoff, Tuch
clothing ✓	Please wear smart clothing at work.	(Be)Kleidung, Kleider
to combine	How can we combine these two ideas?	kombinieren, zusammenfügen
comfortable	I like my clothes to be comfortable.	angenehm, bequem
to concentrate	Concentrate or you'll make a mistake!	sich konzentrieren
consumer	We're all consumers.	Verbraucher/in, Konsument/in
cotton	The shirt is made of cotton.	Baumwolle
dust	There was a lot of dust in the air.	Staub
effect	You can see the effect it has on her.	Auswirkung, Folge
emergency ✓	I need help quickly – it's an emergency!	Notfall
environment	The environment is all around us.	Umwelt
escalator	Take the escalator to the next floor.	Rolltreppe
ethical	It's an ethical question, not just a financial one.	ethisch, moralisch
exporter	Our company is a big exporter to China.	Exporteur
findings	The findings of the research were interesting.	Ergebnisse
to grow	We grow tomatoes in our garden.	(Feldfrucht) anbauen
to harm sb	The gas will harm you if you breathe it in.	jdm schaden
to hold (the line)	Please hold the line.	(*Telefon:*) am Apparat bleiben
illness ✓	He was not at work because of his illness.	Krankheit

import ✓	20% of imports came from China.	Einfuhr
injury	The injury caused him a lot of pain.	Verletzung
label	The brand is on the label of the jeans.	Etikett
litter ✓	Look at all this litter!	Abfall, Müll
medical centre ✓	Five doctors work at the medical centre.	Ärztehaus, medizinisches Zentrum
military service	He did two years' military service.	Militärdienst, Wehrdienst
mood	She's in a strange mood today.	Stimmung, Laune
nostalgia	It's easy to feel nostaligia for the old days.	Nostalgie
ordinary	Those jeans look very ordinary.	gewöhnlich, normal
profit ✓	How much profit did we make last year?	Gewinn
to put sb through	I'll put you through to Mr Jones.	(*Telefon:*) jdn durchstellen
range	They have a wide range of products.	Sortiment, Palette
reply	Send your reply to this email address.	Antwort
retail	I would like to work in retail.	Einzelhandel
robot	Robots work faster than human beings.	Roboter
rubbish ✓	There is a lot of rubbish on the street.	Abfall, Müll
safety guard	Don't forget to use the safety guard!	Schutzblende, Sicherheitsabdeckung
sale ✓	The store has a sale next week.	Schlussverkauf
shopper	The store was full of shoppers.	Käufer/in
soft	This cloth feels very soft.	weich
store ✓	What time does the store close?	Laden, Geschäft
sweater	That sweater looks good on you.	Pullover
to take a message	He's not here today. Can I take a message?	(*Telefon:*) jdm etw ausrichten
various	We tried on various clothes.	verschiedene/r/s
warehouse	The products are stored in a warehouse.	Lager, Lagerhalle
zip	The zip on this jacket is broken.	Reißverschluss

How much have you learned? Do the tasks to find out.
Only look at pages 44–45 if you are stuck.

1 **Lisa and Dan have a small clothes store in Melbourne, Australia. Work out the anagrams and complete the puzzle to find out exactly where it is.**

1 Lisa and Dan worked in LATIRE jobs for years before they started their own store.
2 They like to offer MOUSSNERC good quality for their money.
3 They decided to sell GINTLOCH because they are both interested in fashion.
4 They don't usually have famous brands on the SLEALB of their clothes.
5 However, their clothes are FOOTCRAMELB to wear and they look good.
6 Today they are busy because the store is full of SPOSHREP.
7 Their store is easy to find because it is near the CROTALASE.
8 They hope to make a good TROPFI at the end of the month.
9 They have just put an TANTEDISEVREM in the local newspaper.
10 Soon they will need another delivery from the EWASHORUE.

1 _ _ _ _ _ _
  (1) (2)

2 _ _ _ _ _ _ _ _ _
  (15) (3) (22)

3 _ _ _ _ _ _ _ _
  (4) (7) (16)

4 _ _ _ _ _ _
  (5) (6)

5 _ _ _ _ _ _ _ _ _ _ _
  (11)

6 _ _ _ _ _ _ _ _
  (9) (12)

7 _ _ _ _ _ _ _ _ _
  (17) (20) (21)

8 _ _ _ _ _ _
  (13) (14)

9 _ _ _ _ _ _ _ _ _ _ _ _ _
  (8) (18) (19)

10 _ _ _ _ _ _ _ _ _
  (10)

_ _ _ _ _ _ _ _   _ _ _ _ _ _ _ _
1 2 3 4 5 6 7 8   9 10 11 12 13 14 15 16

_ _ _ _ _ _
17 18 19 20 21 22

2 Find words to match the clues.

1 Your jeans may have one of these or buttons. _ i _

2 Fair and moral behaviour is this. e_ _ _ _ _ _

3 In the modern world we sometimes forget that we can't live without it. _ _ _ _ ron _ _ _ _

4 In one of these, it's important to do the right thing quickly. _ _ _ _ _ _ _ _ y

5 If something isn't interesting or unusual, it's this. o_ _ _ _ _ _ _

6 People leave this behind them (2 possibilities). _ _ tt _ _ , _ _ bb _ _ _

7 If it doesn't come from your country but you can still buy it there, it's one of these. _ _ _ o _ _

8 This is a person or business that sells things to other countries. _ _ _ o _ _ _ _

9 If you carry out a survey, you hope that these will be interesting. _ _ _ _ _ _ _ s

10 This is when there is something wrong with a person's health. _ _ _ _ _ _ s

11 You'll find several doctors here, but it isn't a hospital. _e_ _ _ _ c_ _ _ _ _

12 In several countries, young men have to do this. In Israel, both men and women have to do it. _ _ _ _ _ _ _ y _ _ _ _ _ _e

13 This is how you feel emotionally. _ _ _ d

14 This means 'of several different kinds'. _ _ ri _ _ _

15 When one of these happens, you can buy things cheaply. s _ _ _

16 It can make things very quickly and it doesn't need wages or lunch breaks. r_ _ _ _

17 This is all the goods in a particular brand or a particular store. r _ _ _ _

18 You need to do this or you'll make a mistake. _ _ _ _ _ _ _ _ _ _ e

19 Materials that are this are not natural. _ _ _ _ _ _ _ _ al

20 This is where people should put the answer to number 6. _ _ _

aisle	Would you like an aisle seat or a window seat?	Gang
ancient	The Parthenon is an ancient monument.	alt
announcement	Please listen for further announcements.	Durchsage
balcony	We'd like a room with a balcony.	Balkon
beverage	Beverages must be consumed in the bar area.	Getränk
to board ✓	Please board the aircraft immediately.	an Bord gehen
boarding pass ✓	Please show your boarding pass when you get on the plane.	Bordkarte
cathedral	Cologne has a famous cathedral.	Dom, Kathedrale
cave	It was dark in the cave.	Höhle
century	We're living in the 21st century.	Jahrhundert
to check in	Please check in 90 minutes before the flight.	einchecken, (Gepäck) aufgeben
to confiscate	The teacher might confiscate your mobile phone.	konfiszieren, sicherstellen
counter	You need to go to the counter to buy a ticket.	Schalter
countryside	It's so quiet and green in the countryside.	Land(schaft)
discount	Customers can get a 10% discount.	Rabatt, Nachlass
due to	The delay was due to bad weather.	aufgrund
embassy	Go to the German Embassy to get a new passport.	Botschaft
extra charge	There will be an extra charge for heavy luggage.	Aufschlag, Gebühr
gate ✓	Passengers please go to gate 12.	Flugsteig
greeting	Greetings from Malta!	Gruß
hill ✓	They went for a walk up the hill.	Hügel, Berg
horseback riding (*AE*) ✓	*BE*: horse riding	Reiten (auf dem Pferd)

to improvise	If you forget what to say, just improvise.	improvisieren
to inform	Please inform us if you need to change your reservation.	informieren
introduction	The book's a great introduction to Rome.	Einführung
leisure	What leisure interests do you have?	Freizeit
luckily	Luckily we didn't miss the flight.	glücklicherweise
luggage	Please put labels on all your luggage.	Gepäck
mountainous	Austria is a mountainous country.	bergig
package holiday	Package holidays are often cheaper.	Pauschalreise
palace	The king and queen live in the palace.	Palast
pass	Do you have a pass for the museums?	Eintrittskarte
pie	This apple pie is great!	Kuchen, Torte
plate	Have you finished with your plate?	Teller
to regret	I regret seeing that film – it was terrible!	bedauern
to retire	He retired at the age of 60.	sich zur Ruhe setzen
ruin	After the war, the cathedral was a ruin.	Ruine
scuba diving	I'd love to go scuba diving in the sea.	Gerätetauchen
security	Your bags will be checked by security.	Sicherheitskontrollen, Sicherheitspersonal
sight	What are the most important sights in Malta?	Sehenswürdigkeit
site	This is a historical site.	Stätte, Platz, Schauplatz
sunburn	Careful: don't get a sunburn!	Sonnenbrand
swimsuit	Did you bring your swimsuit?	Badehose, -anzug, Bikini
traveller	This hotel is popular with travellers.	Reisende/r
via	Can we fly to Malta via Rome?	über
walls	The tour of the city walls is at 5 p.m.	Stadtmauer
wet	Unfortunately the weather was wet.	feucht, nass

How much have you learned? Do the tasks to find out.
Only look at pages 48–49 if you are stuck.

1 Find the vowels to complete the missing words.

1 Could I have an ________________ SL seat, please? I don't like sitting near the window.

2 If all you have is that small bag, you don't need to go to the ________________ CNTR. You can use this machine to ________________ CHCK N.

3 My dad said he would never go on a ________________ ________________ PCKG HLDY but when he did, he enjoyed it.

4 What time do we ________________ BRD the flight?

5 Do you think I've got too much ________________ LGGG? We're only going away for three nights.

6 ________________ SCRTY is really strict these days. If you try to take a bottle of drink through, they'll ________________ CNFSCT it.

7 Do we really have to fly to Tenerife ________________ V London? Isn't that the wrong direction?

8 Oh no! I can't find my ________________ ________________ BRDNG PSS: I won't be able to get on the plane!

9 Look at the flight information: we're standing at the wrong ________________ GT for our flight.

10 I'm not exactly an experienced ________________ TRVLLR: I've only been abroad twice in my life.

11 I'm sorry, I didn't understand that last ________________ NNNCMNT. I think my name was mentioned but I didn't get the rest of it.

12 Your rucksack weighs 25 kilos. I'm afraid there will be an ________________ ________________ XTR CHRG for that.

13 We ________________ RGRT to announce that flight LH1242 from Frankfurt to Ibiza has been delayed by six hours.

14 The delay is ________________ ________________ D T bad weather over the Alps.

15 Because of the inconvenience, we will give all our passengers a 10% ________________ DSCNT on their next flight with us.

2 **Complete the crossword.**

1 It's a very big house for very rich people. It usually belongs to the nation now, not to private individuals.
2 It's a hole in the ground. There may be interesting things to see in it.
3 In the old days, they were useful to keep your enemies out of your town. Now tourists like to walk around them.
4 It's a big, important church. Cologne has a famous one.
5 It's another way of saying 'very old'.
6 It can be cheaper to visit museums and other attractions if you buy one of these. (The German word which looks the same has a different meaning!)
7 Don't go swimming without it: you may get into trouble.
8 If you aren't in a town or city or by the sea, this is probably where you are. There may be cows, trees and grass.
9 These are all the things that tourists think they have to see.
10 The Alps are this. So are the Pyrenees. And the Himalayas.
11 It's a building that has partly fallen down. If it's old, tourists often take photos of it.
12 It's easy to get one of these at the beach. It hurts.

to admit	You lied – admit it!	zugeben, eingestehen
adolescence	He started playing football in adolescence.	Jugend, Pubertät
to be fortunate	She was fortunate to get a good education.	sich glücklich schätzen können
to be good at sth	He's good at maths.	etw gut können, gut in etw sein
to be sb's fault	The accident was his fault.	jds Schuld sein, an etw Schuld sein
character	Who's your favourite character in the film?	(*Roman, Film etc.:*) Figur, Person
content	Are you content with your life?	zufrieden
to cope with sth	They were able to cope with the difficulties.	mit etw zurechtkommen
courageous	It was courageous to stand up to the bully.	mutig
to discriminate against sb	The job advert seemed to discriminate against women.	jdn diskriminieren
donation	He gave a donation to help people with AIDS.	Spende
eating disorder	Anorexia is a common eating disorder.	Essstörung
education	It's important to get a good education.	Schulwesen, Bildung(swesen)
final	Is that your final decision?	fertig, endgültig
to force	You can't force me to do it.	zwingen
gender	Both genders must be treated equally.	Geschlecht
generous	That was a generous present.	großzügig
to get away with sth	You won't get away with this crime.	mit etw davonkommen
to get rid of sth	They decided to get rid of their old computer.	etw loswerden
to get sb down	All these problems are getting me down.	jdn deprimieren
glasses ✓	She can't see without her glasses.	Brille
hero ✓	He's my hero. I really admire him.	Held
honest	Be honest: does this dress suit me?	ehrlich

importance	Never forget the importance of education.	Bedeutung, Wichtigkeit
to influence	Through his books, he was able to influence a lot of people.	beeinflussen
inspiring	That was an inspiring story.	inspirierend, anregend
intern	He was an intern in the company for 6 months.	Praktikant/in
learning difficulty	She did well even though she had a learning difficulty.	Lernschwäche, Lernbehinderung
official ✓	That's the official explanation.	offiziell
to pass an exam	She passed all her exams.	eine Prüfung bestehen
polite	That wasn't a polite thing to say.	höflich
principal	If my teacher can't help, I'll go to the principal.	Schuldirektor/in
purpose	What's the purpose of your visit to the USA?	Zweck
to react	How did she react when you said that?	reagieren
role model	A role model doesn't have to be famous.	Vorbild
selfishness	Selfishness is not a good quality.	Egoismus, Selbstsucht
sensible	Stop laughing and be sensible.	vernünftig
to shine	The sun is shining today.	scheinen, glänzen
to succeed	Will she succeed in starting a business?	Erfolg haben
talented	Mozart was very talented.	talentiert
taste	You have good taste in clothes.	Geschmack
technician	The technician will fix the machine.	Techniker/in
to tolerate	We're not friends but we tolerate each other.	tolerieren
transportation	What forms of transportation are best for the environment?	Beförderung
truth	Are you telling the truth?	Wahrheit
value	You can't put a value on friendship.	Wert, Wertvorstellung

How much have you learned? Do the tasks to find out.
Only look at pages 52–53 if you are stuck.

1 **Lucy is talking about her role model, her grandmother Anna. Read the clues and complete the word grid.**

1 She was always …to me and gave me a lot of things – and a lot of attention.
2 She was … – I don't think she was scared of anyone or anything.
3 She was a … artist and could draw very well.
4 It got her … when she was no longer able to see.
5 She taught me that you can … at anything if you believe you can.
6 Through her I learned the … of having someone you can talk to about anything.
7 That can help you to … with things when life is difficult.
8 She was already quite old when I was born, so I was … to have her around for so long.
9 She was … about important things but lied about her age!
10 She had a long life, and although she had some difficult times, I think she was mostly … .
11 She told me always to tell the … – except when there's a good reason not to.
12 Because she grew up in the war, she didn't get much school … .
13 However, she found books … , she read every day.
14 Her advice and the stories she told … me a lot.
15 That taught me the … of talking with older people, not just my peers.

1							G								
2							R								
3							A								
4							N								
5							D								
6							M								
7							O								
8							T								
9							H								
10							E								
11							R								
12							A								
13							N								
14							N								
15							A								

2 **Complete the sentences with the English translations of the words in brackets.**

1 In a job advertisement, you must be careful not to suggest that the position is only for one ______________________. (*Geschlecht*)

2 I'm not sure that I understand the ______________________ of this exercise. What are we trying to achieve? (*Zweck*)

3 During ______________________, children turn into young adults. (*Pubertät*)

4 Does anyone have a ______________________ suggestion about what to do next? (*vernünftig*)

5 Emily ______________________ athletics and other sports. (*gut sein in*)

6 Mr Green is a very good teacher. Perhaps one day he'll become the ______________________. (*Schuldirektor/in*)

7 Will future generations criticize us for ______________________ because of the problems we leave behind? (*Selbstsucht*)

8 I must ______________________, I didn't like that film, although it was very popular. (*zugeben*)

9 How is the new ______________________ doing? Have you introduced her to everyone in the office? (*Praktikant/in*)

10 For me, the real ______________________ are those people who are not afraid to be different. (*Helden*)

11 I'm worried that this office policy ______________________ people with disabilities. (*diskriminieren*)

12 He didn't ______________________ when I said 'Good morning.' Maybe he didn't hear me. (*reagieren*)

13 Your English is very good: I'm sure that you'll ______________________ the exam. (*bestehen*)

14 Actually, very few young people choose celebrities as ______________________. (*Vorbilder*)

15 She's always ______________________ but she's not really friendly. (*höflich*)

16 We've just given a big ______________________ to our favourite charity. (*Spende*)

allergic to	I'm allergic to some foods.	allergisch gegen
annual	Her annual income is a million euros.	jährlich, Jahres-
balanced	Eat a balanced diet, not too much of one thing.	ausgewogen
bill (*BE*)	*AE*: check	Rechnung
to boil	Boil the pasta for 8 minutes.	kochen
cancer	Cancer is an awful disease.	Krebs
chips (*BE*)	*AE*: fries	Pommes frites
to contain	Does this food contain salt?	enthalten
courage	*adj* courageous	Mut
dairy	I'm allergic to some dairy foods.	Milchprodukte
delicious	This cake is delicious!	köstlich
diet	I eat a healthy diet.	Kost, Ernährung
disease	Many diseases can be avoided by a healthy lifestyle.	Erkrankung, Krankheit
dish	How is this dish made?	Gericht
to encourage	The ad encourages healthy eating.	fördern
equipment	Do we have the right equipment for this job?	Ausrüstung
exercise	Professional athletes get a lot of exercise.	Bewegung
to exercise	You should exercise for 30 minutes a day.	sich bewegen
to face sth	We have to face this problem.	vor etw stehen, mit etw zu kämpfen haben
fatty	I don't eat fatty foods.	fettreich
fibre	There is a lot of fibre in wholegrain bread.	Ballaststoffe
fizzy drink	Fizzy drinks often contain sugar.	Erfrischungsgetränk (mit Kohlensäure)
flu	I can't come to school: I've got the flu.	Grippe
fresh	Fresh vegetables are better than frozen ones.	frisch
fried	Don't eat too much fried food.	gebraten
goal	He scored a goal in the football match.	(*Fußball etc.*:) Tor

grade	She's in the ninth grade.	Klasse(nstufe)
immune system	Your immune system fights against disease.	Immunsystem
ingredient	what you need to make a meal	Zutat
leafy vegetables	Most leafy vegetables are green.	Blattgemüse
main course	Will you have a starter and a main course?	Hauptgang
menu ✓	The restaurant has a big menu.	Speisekarte
myth	That's a myth, it isn't true.	Gerücht, Mythos
novel	Have you read the *Twilight* novels?	Roman
nutrient	Good food is full of nutrients.	Nährstoff
nutrition	Nutrition is important for health.	Nahrung, Ernährung
preparation	Is the preparation of this dish difficult?	Zubereitung
rarely	<> often	(nur) selten
relatively	It's relatively quick to prepare.	verhältnismäßig
relaxation	It's important to have time for relaxation.	Entspannung
report	I've read the report.	Reportage
rest	I'm tired. I need a rest.	Erholung, Pause, Ruhe
retired	Now that she's retired she has time for hobbies.	im Ruhestand, pensioniert
saturated	Saturated fats are bad for you.	gesättigt
spicy	I love spicy foods like curry.	würzig, scharf
starchy	Starchy foods include bread and pasta.	stärkehaltig
starter	I'll have a starter before the main course.	Vorspeise
to strengthen	Good food strengthens your immune system.	stärken
to suggest sth	This article suggests chocolate is good for you.	auf etw hindeuten
supplement	Most people don't need supplements.	Zusatz
tasty ✓	This pizza is tasty.	schmackhaft, lecker
unsaturated	I only cook with unsaturated fats.	ungesättigt
whole grain	Whole grain bread is good for you.	Vollkorn

How much have you learned? Do the tasks to find out.
Only look at pages 56–57 if you are stuck.

1 Complete the missing words.

1 Unfortunately I'm _ _ _ _ _ _IC to nuts: I can't eat them.

2 It says on the label that this chocolate 'may _ _ _T_ _ _ nuts', so you shouldn't eat it.

3 I take this _ _ _ _ _ _ _ _ _ _T to improve my health but my doctor says I don't need it if I eat a balanced diet.

4 How can we E_ _ _ _ _ _ _E healthy eating habits in young children?

5 In the winter, a lot of people catch the F_ _ but it's caused by a virus, not the cold weather.

6 It's a _ _ _H that vitamin C pills can prevent colds.

7 I'm reading an interesting N_ _ _L: in it, a virus turns human beings into zombies.

8 The P_ _ _ _ _ _ _ _ _ _ _ of this dish is really easy and quick: it only takes five minutes.

9 My grandfather _ _ _ _ _ _ _ _ _S for at least 30 minutes every day and he's still healthy and strong at the age of 70.

10 Mum _ _ _ _LY eats bread. She says that it doesn't agree with her.

11 Alec is always working: he has no time for _ _ _ _ _A _ _ _ _.

12 Our club had its _ _ _ _ _ _L party last weekend. We have one every year.

13 Hopefully in the future nobody will die from terrible _ _ _ _ _ _ES like cancer and AIDS.

14 When I'm working on the computer, I try to have a _ _ _T every hour. Otherwise, my eyes get tired.

15 Our Super-Vitamin Pills will _ _ _ _NG_ _ _ _ our immune system.

16 The findings of the study _ _ _ _ _ _T that many teenagers don't have good diets.

2 **Find the nutrition and food words in the word square. Write the German meaning next to each word.**

8 adjectives

____________________ ____________________

____________________ ____________________

____________________ ____________________

____________________ ____________________

____________________ ____________________

____________________ ____________________

____________________ ____________________

____________________ ____________________

6 nouns

____________________ ____________________

____________________ ____________________

____________________ ____________________

____________________ ____________________

____________________ ____________________

____________________ ____________________

C	T	N	T	B	W	A	F	I	B	R	E	C	D
U	A	E	S	A	S	L	E	A	F	Y	O	H	I
S	S	D	E	L	I	C	I	O	U	S	C	I	E
A	T	A	L	A	L	R	E	T	S	A	E	C	T
T	Y	A	I	N	G	R	E	D	I	E	N	T	D
U	R	H	E	C	H	A	R	G	T	M	E	N	D
R	D	P	V	E	G	E	T	A	B	L	E	T	T
A	A	I	L	D	S	F	R	I	D	G	F	S	S
T	I	F	A	T	T	Y	S	I	N	C	I	E	T
E	R	L	O	S	M	O	D	I	S	H	Z	S	A
D	Y	R	E	B	C	R	I	P	S	P	Z	P	R
S	S	T	A	R	C	H	Y	T	E	S	Y	E	T

application form	Please fill in the application form.	Antragsformular
to apply sth	We should apply what we've learned.	etw anwenden
approach	Do you think that this is the best approach?	Herangehensweise, Ansatz
average	The average German uses 193 litres of water a day.	Durchschnitt(s-), durchschnittlich
to benefit from sth	Consumers will benefit from lower prices.	von etw profitieren
biofuel	Is biofuel the solution to the energy crisis?	Biokraftstoff
to blame sb/sth	There is no point in blaming anyone.	jdm/einer Sache die Schuld geben
compost bin	Put the remaining food in the compost bin.	Komposttonne, Kompostierfass
container	Put it in this container.	Behälter, Behältnis
convinced	I'm convinced that we can succeed.	überzeugt
crisis	If we do nothing, the problem will become a crisis.	Krise
to cycle	I cycle to work most days.	(mit dem) Fahrrad fahren
disappointment	The film was a real disappointment.	Enttäuschung
disaster	Climate change will be a disaster for many people.	Katastrophe
environmental	She's an environmental activist.	Umwelt-
environmentally friendly	We use environmentally friendly products.	umweltfreundlich
everyday	'Climate change' has become an everyday expression.	Alltags-
fossil fuels	Coal, oil and gas are fossil fuels.	fossile Brennstoffe
heating	We need energy for heating and light.	Heizung
to highlight	This highlights the problem with your suggestion.	hervorheben, verdeutlichen
issue	Climate change is an important issue.	Frage, Streitpunkt, Problem

key	This is one of the key things to consider.	wichtigste/r/s, Haupt-
to melt	The ice is melting in Antarctica.	schmelzen
movement	He is involved with the environmental movement.	Bewegung
negativity	<> positivity	negative Einstellung
nuclear power plant	Will they shut down the nuclear power plant?	Atomkraftwerk
politician	The politician promised to change the law.	Politiker/in
to power sth	Solar panels power my computer.	etw mit Strom versorgen
progress	Are we making progress with the project?	Fortschritt(e)
to re-use	Repair, re-use or recycle.	wiederverwenden
resort	They stayed at a ski resort.	Ferienort
roof	The activists climbed up to the roof.	Dach
salary	My salary has gone down this year.	Lohn, Gehalt
scenery	Let's just sit here and enjoy the scenery.	Landschaft, Kulisse
shy	She's shy with people she doesn't know.	schüchtern
solar panel	We get our electricity from solar panels.	Solarzelle
supervisor	If you want more money, talk with your supervisor.	Vorgesetzte/r
to survive	Will humans survive climate change?	überleben
sustainable	We need sustainable sources of energy.	nachhaltig
to switch off	Don't forget to switch off the light.	ausschalten, ausmachen
to take action	It's time to take action.	tätig werden, Maßnahmen ergreifen
timetable	The timetable says our train goes at 5.30.	Fahrplan
vocational school	school which prepares sb for work life	Berufs(fach)schule
to warn	I warned you not to do that.	(davor) warnen
waste	There is no waste in nature: everything is re-used.	Abfall

How much have you learned? Do the tasks to find out.
Only look at pages 60–61 if you are stuck.

1 **Complete the crossword.**

1 The scientists are making … on developing new energy sources.
2 We can't wait for governments and … to solve the world's problems.
3 The problem will get worse and become a … if we don't do something soon.
4 Our neighbours' car is … by electricity: it doesn't need petrol or diesel.
5 Do you think that the … person in Britain cares about the environment?
6 The … panels on our roof provide all of our energy.
7 We often say that things are 'green' if they are to do with the … movement: green energy, green values, etc.
8 Organic farming is … : it uses no dangerous chemicals and less fossil fuel.
9 Rudy's story … the importance of positive thinking.
10 The students discussed the … with their teacher and found a good solution.
11 Modern industry creates a lot of … . Isn't there a way to recycle it?
12 Will the polar bears … or will they all die?
13 We can make … from plants and put it in our cars instead of fossil fuels.
14 It's a good idea to … off your mobile phone in class.

2 **Find the vowels to complete the missing words.**

1 Some people are still not ____________________ that climate change is caused by human beings. CNVNCD

2 Don't ____________________ other people for the problem, because we all caused it. BLM

3 We're all addicted to ____________________ ____________________, even though we know that they are bad for us and the environment. FSSL FLS

4 How can we ____________________ these materials instead of throwing them away? R-S

5 If you aren't sure how to do the job, ask your ____________________ for more training. SPRVSR

6 This isn't working: maybe we should try a different ____________________. PPRCH

7 In northern Europe, ____________________ uses a lot of power because the weather is cold a lot of the time. HTNG

8 Isn't it more important to have an interesting job than a big ____________________? Money isn't everything, you know. SLRY

9 We have talked about this for long enough. It's time to ____________________ ____________________ now. TK CTN

10 It's an ____________________ problem – everyone has it at some time. VRYDY

11 The course was a ____________________ : it wasn't as good as they expected. DSPPNTMNT

12 These products are ____________________ ____________________, so it's safe to use them. NVRNMNTLLY FRNDLY

13 Please put the food in the ____________________ ____________________. Don't just throw it away. CMPST BN

14 I take my sandwiches to school in a re-usable ____________________, not in a plastic bag. CNTNR

15 We all ____________________ from modern technology so we don't want to get rid of it. BNFT

16 We learned about the world of work when we went to ____________________ ____________________. VCTNL SCHL

Unit 1

1 **1** conversation; **2** communicate; **3** map; **4** native; **5** chat; **6** fluent; **7** translation; **8** pronounce; **9** home; **10** foreign; **11** appointment; **12** celebrate

2 **1** directions; **2** customers; **3** entrance; **4** advertising; **5** stairs; **6** voice; **7** Nowadays; **8** department; **9** capital city; **10** reason; **11** practise; **12** population; **13** canteen; **14** manufacturing; **15** accent; **16** pronunciation; **17** present; **18** purse; **19** series; **20** advantage

Unit 2

1 **1** refugees; **2** war; **3** asylum; **4** passports; **5** immigrants; **6** welcome; **7** criticize; **8** background; Paul's dream is to become a: German citizen

2 **10 words about family:** adopted – *adoptiert*; relative – *Verwandte/r*; stepmother – *Stiefmutter*; uncle – *Onkel*; grandparent – *Großelternteil*; sibling – *Bruder oder Schwester*; husband – *Ehemann*; wife – *Ehefrau*; aunt – *Tante*; surname – *Nachname*
4 words about the world of work: colleague – *Kollege/Kollegin*; company – *Firma*; meeting – *Sitzung, Besprechung*; advertisement – *Werbespot*

A	S	T	R	A	W	I	F	E	D	R	I	S
R	I	G	R	A	N	D	P	A	R	E	N	T
M	B	R	A	D	K	R	I	L	L	U	U	E
E	L	I	C	O	M	P	A	N	Y	N	T	P
E	I	G	U	P	U	P	Y	S	H	C	R	M
T	N	H	R	T	R	O	L	U	F	L	W	O
I	G	U	D	E	D	F	I	R	E	E	R	T
N	O	N	S	D	R	A	U	N	T	E	E	H
G	I	D	D	L	R	E	L	A	T	I	V	E
A	H	U	S	B	A	N	D	M	A	W	I	R
A	D	V	E	R	T	I	S	E	M	E	N	T
W	O	R	C	O	L	L	E	A	G	U	E	D

Unit 3

1 **three adjectives:** comfortable – *bequem*, tight – *eng*, smart – *schick*
two verbs: fit – *passen*, wear – *tragen*
six nouns: suit – *Anzug*, fashion – *Mode*, jacket – *Jacke*, leather – *Leder*, shirt – *Hemd*, sunglasses – *Sonnenbrille*

2 **1** down; **2** after; **3** up; **4** about; **5** up; **6** away; **7** down; **8** out

3 **1** ban; **2** improve; **3** silly; **4** career; **5** mobile/cell phone; **6** save; **7** lyrics; **8** cause; **9** serious; **10** cheap; **11** earn; **12** tastes

Unit 4

1 1 upload; 2 privacy; 3 comment; 4 account; 5 media; 6 delete; 7 cyberbullying; 8 users; 9 networks; 10 message

2 1 upset; 2 insecure; 3 embarrassing; 4 annoyed; 5 remove; 6 depressed; 7 employer; 8 complain; 9 advice; 10 contact

3 1 programme; 2 public; 3 lies; 4 bored; 5 choice; 6 diary; 7 joke; 8 insult; 9 stranger; 10 youth

Unit 5

1 1 performance; 2 celebrity; 3 fame; 4 TV show; 5 contestant; 6 prize; 7 scandal; 8 successful; 9 glamorous; 10 rehab; 11 drugs; 12 headlines; 13 tragic; 14 secretly; A lot of Hollywood actors have: plastic surgery

2 **Two verbs:** change – *umsteigen*; depart – *abfahren*
Five nouns: ticket machine – *Fahrkartenautomat*; journey – *Fahrt, Reise*; seat – *Platz, Sitz*; trip – *Reise*; platform – *Bahnsteig, Gleis*
Six nouns for people and things you find there: furniture – *Möbel*; shelves – *Regale*; keyboard – *Tastatur*; stationery – *Schreibwaren*; trainee – *Auszubildende/r*; printer – *Drucker*

G	E	A	T	T	R	I	P	A	N	T	H	O
J	R	R	U	I	Z	D	E	P	A	R	T	F
O	I	T	F	C	S	H	E	L	V	E	S	U
U	C	H	J	K	M	A	R	G	A	R	E	R
R	K	U	K	E	Y	B	O	A	R	D	N	N
N	P	L	A	T	F	O	R	M	E	M	I	I
E	G	R	E	M	G	R	O	Y	S	A	D	T
Y	P	S	T	A	T	I	O	N	E	R	Y	U
S	A	L	L	C	Y	M	A	D	A	G	E	R
U	L	F	R	H	I	C	H	A	T	R	L	E
S	T	R	A	I	N	E	E	S	Y	L	V	I
A	N	D	R	N	E	C	H	A	N	G	E	W
W	I	L	F	E	R	P	R	I	N	T	E	R

Unit 6

1 1 vocational college; 2 start a company; 3 disadvantage; 4 training; 5 fluent; 6 voluntary; 7 primary / elementary school; 8 parents; 9 secondary / high school; 10 promoted; 11 work placement; 12 childhood; 13 come true; 14 prediction; 15 certificate

2 **1** achievement; **2** experience; **3** goal; **4** employ; **5** waste; **6** dreamer; **7** build; **8** risk

3 **1** apply; **2** outdoors; **3** bully; **4** afford; **5** success; **6** matter; **7** possibility; **8** Interviewees

Unit 7

1 **1** analytical; **2** artistic; **3** communicative; **4** excellent; **5** exciting; **6** industrial; **7** innovative; **8** reliable; **9** financial; **10** outgoing; **11** responsible; **12** common; **13** strict

2 **1** profession; **2** childminding; **3** caregiver; **4** artist; **5** mechanics; **6** construction; **7** driver; **8** programmer

3 **1** careers counsellor; **2** computer science; **3** covering letter; **4** further education; **5** job advertisement; **6** technically minded; **7** tour guide

Unit 8

1 **1** abroad; **2** apprenticeship; **3** diversity; **4** opportunities; **5** application; **6** temporary; **7** contract; **8** permanently; **9** relocate; **10** unfamiliar;
Fabian wants to work in the Republic of Ireland

2 **1** administrative; **2** complaint; **3** dissatisfied; **4** enthusiastic; **5** examination; **6** excited; **7** graph; **8** habit; **9** knowledge; **10** machinery; **11** majority; **12** percentage; **13** strength; **14** stressful

3 **1** operate; **2** predict; **3** regret; **4** draw; **5** have; **6** overcome; **7** work; **8** adapt

Unit 9

1 **1** violence; **2** victim; **3** solution; **4** shoot; **5** offend; **6** prevent; **7** murder; **8** attack; **9** trouble; **10** murderer; **11** crime; **12** cause; **13** guns; **14** realise

2 **1** enemies; **2** brilliant; **3** justify; **4** beliefs; **5** uncomfortable; **6** lifestyle; **7** racism; **8** ignorance; **9** cancel; **10** charity; **11** illustrate; **12** judge; **13** persuade; **14** disability

Unit 10

1 **4 adjectives:** addictive – *süchtig*; risky – *riskant*; irresponsible – *verantwortungslos*; terrifying – *furchterregend*
3 nouns for actions: speed – *Geschwindigkeit*; shoplifting – *Ladendiebstahl*; adventure – *Abenteuer*
2 nouns for consequences: overdose – *Überdosis*; accident – *Unfall*
3 verbs: vandalize – *verwüsten*; injure – *verletzen*; ruin – *zugrunde richten*

M	E	M	T	E	R	R	I	F	Y	I	N	G	A
S	B	E	R	O	V	E	R	D	O	S	E	T	D
H	R	S	H	I	P	A	P	P	L	I	C	A	V
O	I	R	R	E	S	P	O	N	S	I	B	L	E
P	S	I	O	N	P	E	R	P	M	E	N	T	N
L	K	M	A	C	S	P	E	E	D	M	I	A	T
I	Y	A	D	D	I	C	T	I	V	E	L	T	U
F	I	V	A	N	D	A	L	I	Z	E	O	P	R
T	N	U	L	T	F	O	O	P	I	R	H	O	E
I	T	U	R	E	M	A	C	C	I	D	E	N	T
N	U	V	I	C	O	I	N	J	U	R	E	B	O
G	R	U	I	N	E	L	B	O	U	R	N	E	X

2 **1** affect; **2** health and safety; **3** criminal record; **4** Entrepreneurs; **5** embarrass; **6** depends on; **7** law; **8** obvious; **9** property; **10** prove; **11** unemployment; **12** human beings; **13** increases; **14** peers; **15** recent; **16** criticism

Unit 11

1 **1** retail; **2** consumers; **3** clothing; **4** labels; **5** comfortable; **6** shoppers; **7** escalator; **8** profit; **9** advertisement; **10** warehouse; The clothes store is in Eastland Shopping Centre

2 **1** zip; **2** ethical; **3** environment; **4** emergency; **5** ordinary; **6** litter, rubbish; **7** import; **8** exporter; **9** findings; **10** illness; **11** medical centre; **12** military service; **13** mood; **14** various; **15** sale; **16** robot; **17** range; **18** concentrate; **19** artificial; **20** bin

Unit 12

1 **1** aisle; **2** counter, check in; **3** package holiday; **4** board; **5** luggage; **6** security, confiscate; **7** via; **8** boarding pass; **9** gate; **10** traveller; **11** announcement; **12** extra charge; **13** regret; **14** due to; **15** discount

2 **1** palace; **2** cave; **3** walls; **4** cathedral; **5** ancient; **6** pass; **7** swimsuit; **8** countryside; **9** sights; **10** mountainous; **11** ruin; **12** sunburn

Unit 13

1 **1** generous; **2** courageous; **3** talented; **4** down; **5** succeed; **6** importance; **7** cope; **8** fortunate; **9** honest; **10** content; **11** truth; **12** education; **13** inspiring; **14** influenced; **15** value

2 **1** gender; **2** purpose; **3** adolescence; **4** sensible; **5** is good at; **6** principal; **7** selfishness; **8** admit; **9** intern; **10** heroes; **11** discriminates against; **12** react; **13** pass; **14** role models; **15** polite; **16** donation

Unit 14

1 **1** allergic; **2** contain; **3** supplement; **4** encourage; **5** flu; **6** myth; **7** novel; **8** preparation; **9** exercises; **10** rarely; **11** relaxation; **12** annual; **13** diseases; **14** rest; **15** strengthen; **16** suggest

2 **8 adjectives:** balanced – *ausgewogen*; delicious – *lecker*; fatty – *fettreich*; fizzy – *mit Kohlensäure*; leafy – *Blatt-*; saturated – *gesättigt*; starchy – *stärkehaltig*; tasty – *schmackhaft, lecker*
6 nouns: dairy – *Milchprodukte*; diet – *Kost, Ernährung*; dish – *Gericht*; fibre – *Ballaststoffe*; ingredient – *Zutat*; vegetable – *Gemüse*

C	T	N	T	B	W	A	F	I	B	R	E	C	D
U	A	E	S	A	S	L	E	A	F	Y	O	H	I
S	S	D	E	L	I	C	I	O	U	S	C	I	E
A	T	A	L	A	L	R	E	T	S	A	E	C	T
T	Y	A	I	N	G	R	E	D	I	E	N	T	D
U	R	H	E	C	H	A	R	G	T	M	E	N	D
R	D	P	V	E	G	E	T	A	B	L	E	T	T
A	A	I	L	D	S	F	R	I	D	G	F	S	S
T	I	F	A	T	T	Y	S	I	N	C	I	E	T
E	R	L	O	S	M	O	D	I	S	H	Z	S	A
D	Y	R	E	B	C	R	I	P	S	P	Z	P	R
S	S	T	A	R	C	H	Y	T	E	S	Y	E	T

Unit 15

1 **1** progress; **2** politicians; **3** crisis; **4** powered; **5** average; **6** solar; **7** environmental; **8** sustainable; **9** highlights; **10** issue; **11** waste; **12** survive; **13** biofuel; **14** switch

2 **1** convinced; **2** blame; **3** fossil fuels; **4** re-use; **5** supervisor; **6** approach; **7** heating; **8** salary; **9** take action; **10** everyday; **11** disappointment; **12** environmentally friendly; **13** compost bin; **14** container; **15** benefit; **16** vocational school